GAME ON!

CHECKERS
FOR BEGINNERS

JON TREMAINE

WINDMILL
BOOKS

INTRODUCTION

Checkers was played by the ancient pharaohs dating back to 1500 BCE. The rules have changed very little since then.

Today, checkers is taken very seriously and international competitions take place regularly.

The checkers grand master Marion Tinsley is considered to be the greatest checkers player that ever lived. He never lost a championship game and only lost seven games in his checkers career. Two of his losses were to a very smart computer program! Marion was mentored by Asa Long, who was a checkers grand master for 70 years.

Checkers can be played at all levels, and its simple rules can be grasped by everyone.

You can learn certain set moves in checkers.
A winning strategy may take you longer to learn, but
you will have a lot of fun practicing. Read on to learn
some amazing checkers skills.

Good luck!

THE BOARD

The board is identical to a chess board: 8 x 8 squares, alternately checkered light and dark. The two players are known as black and red. Players sit opposite each other with the board between them. They must make sure there is a light square in the lower right corner.

BLACK

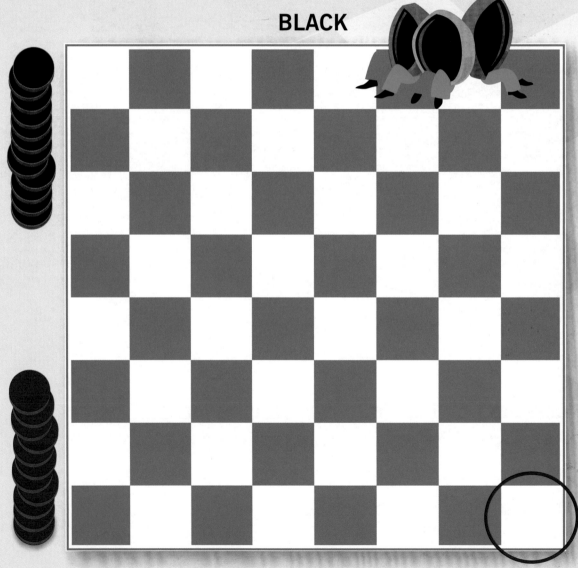

RED

THE SETUP

Each player has 12 circular pieces, made of either wood or plastic. To begin, the pieces are arranged in the first three rows, like this:

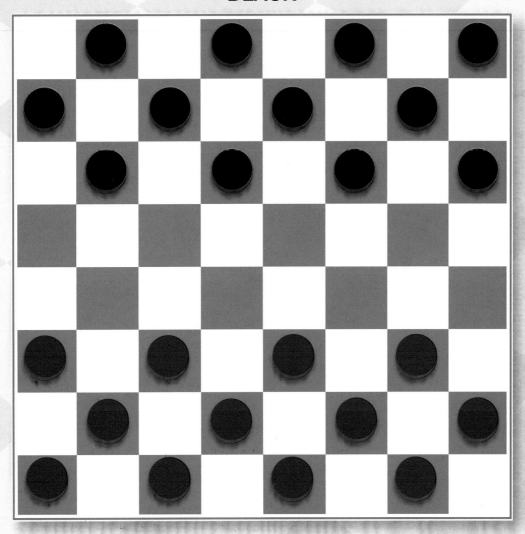

BLACK

RED

NOTATION

Play only takes place on the dark-colored squares, and for ease of explanation we have numbered the squares from 1–32, like this:

BLACK

	1		2		3		4
5		6		7		8	
	9		10		11		12
13		14		15		16	
	17		18		19		20
21		22		23		24	
	25		26		27		28
29		30		31		32	

RED

OBJECT OF THE GAME

The object of the game is to capture as many of your opponent's pieces as you can. You either need to capture all their pieces or try to stop them from being able to move their pieces.

BLACK

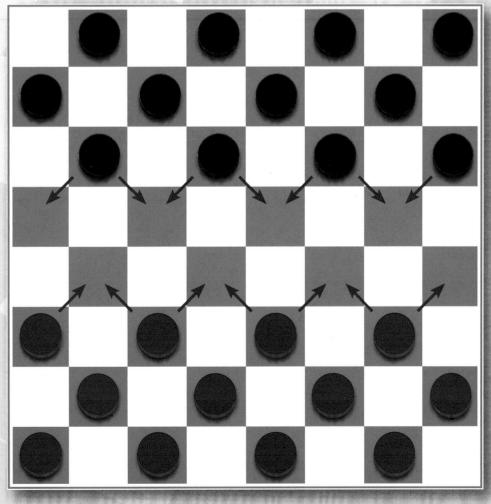

RED

THE PLAY

Black always starts the game. Play then alternates between the two players. The pieces are moved diagonally: one space at a time (except when capturing), always in a forward direction, and always on the dark-colored squares.

BLACK

RED

TOUCH AND MOVE

If you need to adjust a piece on the board that is overlapping its square, you must first tell your opponent what you are about to do. Otherwise, you must move the first piece that you touch. If you touch an unplayable piece (accidentally or deliberately), you will receive a warning. If you repeat the move, you will forfeit the game.

CAPTURING

You capture a piece by leapfrogging over it onto the next vacant square. The piece that you have just jumped over is then removed from the board.

You can capture more than one of your opponent's pieces in one move if the situation allows. In this picture, you can continue to move because there is a space to land and another red to capture.

HUFFING

If it is possible to capture a piece, you must do it. In the past, if you failed to make a possible capture, your opponent could "huff" you. Huffing meant that they could remove your piece from the board and carry out their own move. Modern-day play has scrapped this rule. Your opponent can now only insist that you make the capturing move and that you take back the illegal move you have just made. If you have two possible capture moves, you can choose which one you want to make.

CROWNING

As you capture your opponent's pieces, you should also attempt to reach your opponent's back row. If you succeed, your piece immediately becomes a king! You signify its elevated stature by placing one of your captured pieces on top. This is called "crowning" the king.

King pieces are all-powerful. They can still only move one diagonal square at a time, but they can do it in either direction – forward or backward!

A king can wreak havoc on the opposition. It is possible to have more than one king. You can launch a formidable attack in this way.

BLACK

RED

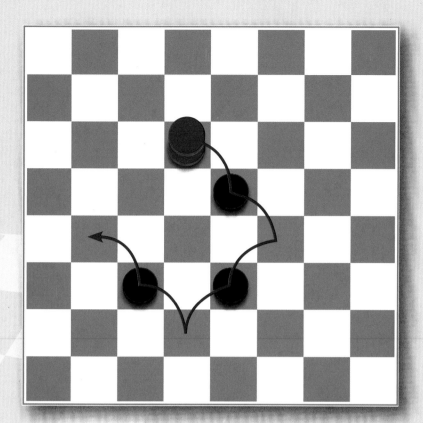

A king can also change direction when capturing.

Remember, though— a lowly checkers piece can still capture a king!

DRAWS

Drawn games happen quite often. If both players agree, a draw can be called at any time in the game.

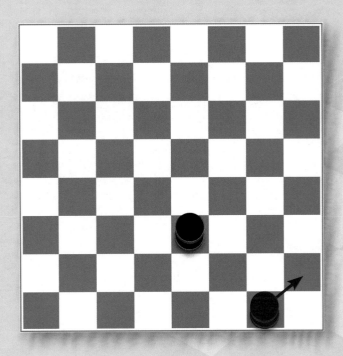

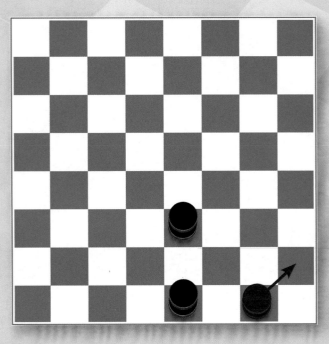

STALEMATE

A stalemate occurs when the players are left with just one king each – all other pieces having been captured. Each player now has 40 moves to try to win. If both players fail, the game is declared a draw.

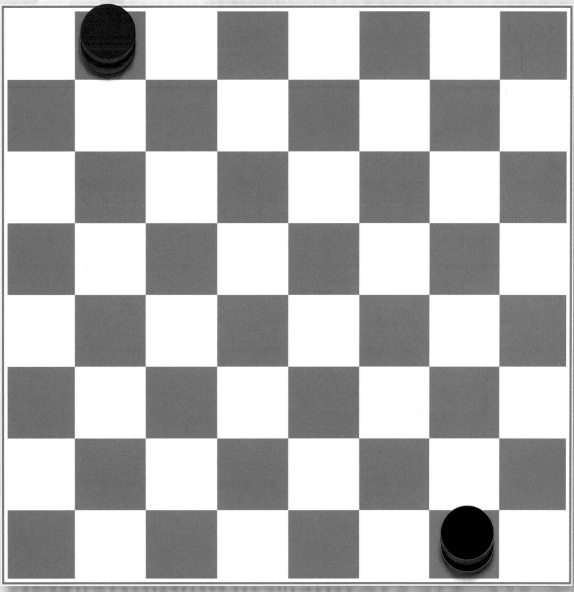

STRATEGY

Here are some playing hints and a few traps to avoid. Follow the moves on the checkerboard below and you will soon get the hang of things.

	1		2		3		4
5		6		7		8	
	9		10		11		12
13		14		15		16	
	17		18		19		20
21		22		23		24	
	25		26		27		28
29		30		31		32	

OPENING MOVES

Black always starts and has seven possible moves. The best opening move is 11–15.

In order of strength, the opening moves are: 11–15, 9–14, 11–16, 10–15, 12–16, 10–14, 9–13.

Red's best reponses to black's opening moves are:

If black plays 11–15, red responds with 23–19 or 23–28 or 22-18.

If black plays 9–14, red responds with 22–18 or 22–17.

If black plays 11–16, red responds with 22–18 or 24–19.

If black plays 10–15, red responds with 21–17.

If black plays 12–16, red responds with 24–20.

If black plays 10–14, red responds with 22–17 or 24–19.

If black plays 9–13, red responds with 22–18.

BLOCKING

This is a subtle technique that forces a player to move in a certain way. To practice, set up your board like this. It is red's move...

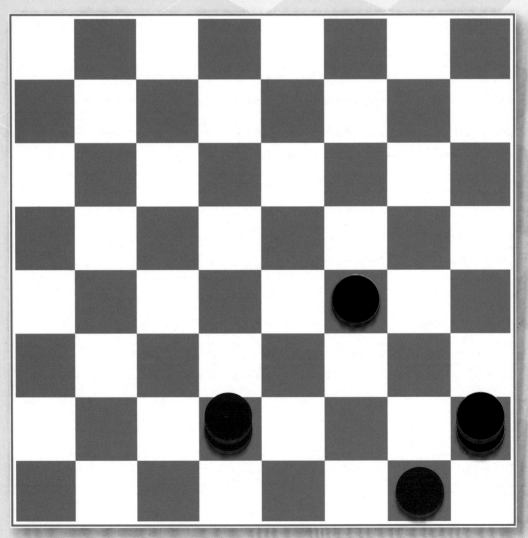

Follow these moves on your board:

BLACK	RED
	32-27
28-32	27-24
19-28 (mandatory)	26-23 (red wins)

Black is tangled up with nowhere to go!

	1		2		3		4
5		6		7		8	
	9		10		11		12
13		14		15		16	
	17		18		19		20
21		22		23		24	
	25		26		27		28
29		30		31		32	

TRAPS

Here is a classic trap to look out for. Black's fate is sealed after only six moves!

Follow this on your board:

BLACK	RED
11-15	24-20
8-11	28-24
9-13	23-19
4-8	20-16
11-20	22-17
13-22	25-4

Position of pieces after black plays 4–8:

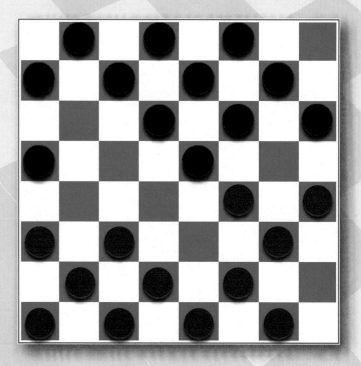

**Red captures
three pieces and
becomes a king!**

TWO AGAINST ONE

A game is often reduced to two kings against one. The two kings will always win, but the win can sometimes be quite difficult to achieve. The most effective technique is shown here (with red having the two kings):

	BLACK	RED
1.	32–28	24–27
2.	28–32	19–23
3.	32–28	27–32
4.	28–24	32–28
5.	24–20	23–18
6.	20–16	18–15
7.	16–20	15–11

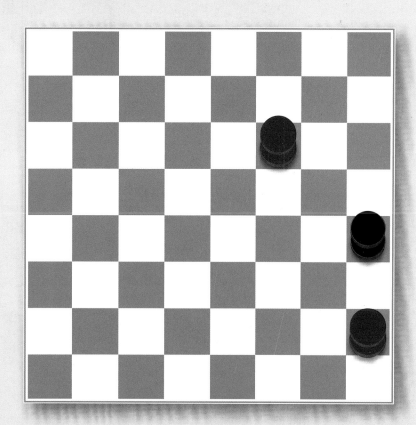

Remember this move – it's very useful!

THE DOUBLE CORNER

Look at the board below. If it is black's move, his king must retreat, and will eventually be trapped at the edge of the board and lose the game. If it is red's move, he would also have to retreat, but by heading for his "double corner" (squares 28 & 32) he will be able to force a draw. Black will find it impossible to beat him. Red will just keep moving from 28–32, 32–28, 28–32, and so on, until the "40 move" rule kicks in.

BLACK

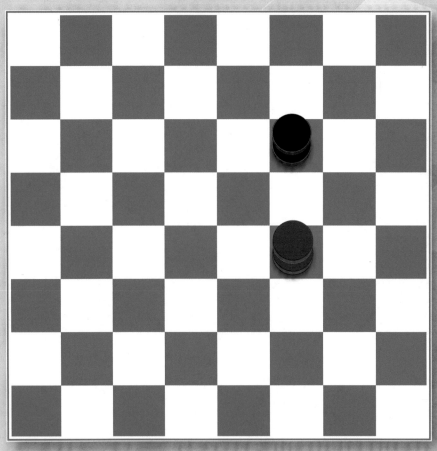

RED

ANTI-CHECKERS

This amusing variation of checkers is a lot of fun to play. The object of "Anti-Checkers" is simply to be the first person to lose all your pieces! You strive to put your pieces in peril at every opportunity.

12-MAN DIAGONAL

This is another interesting variation that you might like to try. If you are using 12 pieces per person, the board will be set up like this:

Pieces are crowned if they reach any of the four squares marked with an arrow. Apart from this, the rules remain the same as for ordinary checkers.

9-MAN DIAGONAL

This is a fast and furious version of Diagonal Checkers. Only 9 pieces are used per side, and crowning only occurs on the three squares indicated. You really have to think quickly for this one!

TOP 10 TIPS

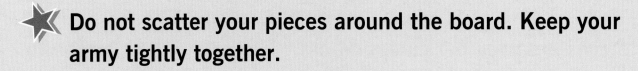

- Do not scatter your pieces around the board. Keep your army tightly together.

- Play toward the center, avoid the sides.

- Don't advance too many pieces to start with – play steadily.

- Direct your attack toward the double corners.

- Try to force your pieces forward so they can become kings.

- If you have to sacrifice a piece, make sure you don't accidentally give away two, or even three!

- If red still occupies 32, black must avoid entering 28 at all costs, as shown on the next page.

- If black still occupies 1, red should avoid square 5.

- Immediately bring your kings back into play – don't leave them sitting in the back row.

- Make sure that you don't give away more pieces than you get back!

DOUBLE CORNER

DOUBLE CORNER

PRACTICE MAKES PERFECT

The only way to get better is to practice! When you start to feel confident, you could make the game more exciting by having a time limit. Each player has a certain amount of time to make all their moves. If you run out of time, you lose the game! Why not stage a mini-tournament for your friends?

Published in 2022 by Windmill Books,
an Imprint of Rosen Publishing
29 East 21st Street, New York, NY 10010

Copyright © 2022 iSeek Ltd.

Cataloging-in-Publication Data

Names: Tremaine, Jon.
Title: Checkers for beginners / Jon Tremaine.
Description: New York : Windmill Books, 2022. | Series: Game on!
Identifiers: ISBN 9781538270059 (pbk.) | ISBN 9781538270073 (library bound) |
ISBN 9781538270066 (6 pack) | ISBN 9781538270080 (ebook)
Subjects: LCSH: Board games–Juvenile literature.
Classification: LCC GV1312.T75 2022 | DDC 794–dc23

Manufactured in the United States of America

CPSIA Compliance Information: Batch BSWM22: For Further Information contact Rosen Publishing, New York, New York at 1-800-237-9932